I Will See You in Heaven

Friar Jack Wintz

PARACLETE PRESS

BREWSTER, MASSACHUSETTS

I Will See You in Heaven

2014 First Printing This Edition
2010 First Printing Original Edition

Copyright © 2010, 2014 by Jack Wintz

ISBN: 978-1-61261-584-4

The Library of Congress has catalogued the first edition of this book as follows:
        Library of Congress Cataloging-in-Publication Data
    Wintz, Jack. I will see you in heaven / Jack Wintz.
        p. cm.
    ISBN 978-1-55725-732-1
        1. Animals—Religious aspects—Christianity. 2. Pets—Religious aspects—Christianity. 3. Future life—Christianity. I. Title. BT746.W55 2010
        231.7—dc22   2009053415

10 9 8 7 6 5 4 3 2 1

Published by Paraclete Press
Brewster, Massachusetts
www.paracletepress.com
Printed in the United States of America

*This book is written for
the millions of people
who love their animal companions.
All may find inspiration here.*

I Will See You in Heaven is also designed to help those who have recently lost a pet by keeping it in loving remembrance. You may want to use the following Presentation Page.

Presented to

_____

By _____

In Loving Remembrance of

_____

On This Day

_____

Contents

Introduction

We have a deep desire to know if we will see our pets again, and all the other lovely creatures alongside whom we now inhabit this planet. What will become of them after they die?

A friend of mine once told me the following story:

Anne lives in Cincinnati, where a few years ago she faced the important questions of death and eternity as she was present at the death of her dearly loved dog, Miss Daisy. Anne had befriended Miss Daisy ten years earlier when the dog, of mixed Spaniel origin, was barely one year old. With the help of her adult son, Anne rescued Miss Daisy from Cincinnati's inner city.

"I would see her wandering around the neighborhood where I worked at an elementary school," Anne told me. "I came to realize that she was obviously a stray and lost— and she was adorable! I took cans of tuna to the area where Miss Daisy hung out, but she was very afraid of people and wouldn't approach the tuna till she was left alone. My rescue attempts went on for many months."

In time, Anne was successful in winning Miss Daisy's confidence and was able to take her to her home.

"Miss Daisy was still very shy," Anne told me, "but she eventually became a loyal and loving member of our family. Realizing that Miss Daisy needed a companion, I went to the dog pound and came home with a dog named Andy. For ten years or so, Miss Daisy and Andy were very happy companions, and both became cherished members of the family. But I became especially attached to Miss Daisy.

"Eventually, Miss Daisy became ill, and we had to make the very difficult decision to have her 'put down.' My son and I took her to the veterinarian so he could put her to sleep. We wanted the vet to come out to our car so Miss Daisy would be in familiar surroundings and we could be holding her, but he refused our request. So we had to take her inside. We laid her on the vet's table on her special blanket. We petted Miss Daisy gently and spoke softly to her as the vet got everything ready to give her the injection. Miss Daisy lay there quietly for a few seconds, and then, just before the injection took effect, she lifted her head and looked directly into my eyes. I can still see that look. It was as if she knew what was going on and she was saying good-bye."

Anne recalls how her heart melted, and to this day tears come to her eyes when she remembers that scene. "I still miss the loving pet who had been my dear friend for so many years. *I know I will see Miss Daisy again!"*

I'm sure that most of us have our own memories of being profoundly grief-stricken at the death of a beloved pet. These are not childish concerns, but the mature reflections of loving Christians.

Many of us prefer to pose the question "Will I see my dog in heaven?" in broader spiritual terms. There is more involved in this question than simply wondering if we will ever be reunited with a loved animal. For instance, does God's plan of salvation include only humans, or does it include animals, too? In even broader terms, does God intend the *whole* created world to be saved?

As a Franciscan friar for over fifty years, I am familiar with the stories of St. Francis of Assisi and his close relationship with animals, and these stories have informed the way that I view these things. Perhaps you've heard the stories of this brown-robed friar preaching to the birds, releasing Brother

Rabbit from a trap, or letting Sister Raven serve as his "alarm clock" to awaken him for early morning prayer. I've known for a long time that historians have credited Francis with composing one of the first great poems in the Italian language—a poem, or hymn, usually entitled *The Canticle of the Creatures*. In this hymn, sometimes known as *The Canticle of Brother Sun*, Francis invites all his brother and sister creatures to praise their Creator—Brother Sun and Sister Moon, Brother Fire and Sister Water, as well as Sister Earth, our mother, with all her various fruits and vividly colored flowers.

Some thirty years ago I came to the conclusion, which I've never abandoned, that St. Francis came to see that all creatures form one family of creation. Maybe that conclusion is obvious to you, but for me this idea dawned quite gradually. The conviction has grown stronger and stronger, and this book has grown out of that conviction, and explores the implications of it. What would it mean if all creatures were one family? How would it affect us? How would it change our understanding about God, and about how we relate to God and to each other?

Three Prayers of Blessing

FOR ANY ANIMAL, FISH, BIRD, OR OTHER CREATURE

SCRIPTURE REFLECTION

[Christ] is before all things,
and in him all things hold together. —Col. 1:17

Gather your family and friends together for these blessings
—it is good to have as much of the family of God present as possible.
Insert the name of your animal companion into these prayers.

For Any of God's Creatures

Blessed are you, Lord God,
Maker of all living creatures.
On the fifth and sixth days of creation,
   you called forth fish in the sea,
   birds in the air, and animals on the land.
You inspired St. Francis to call all animals
   his brothers and sisters.
We ask you to bless this animal (these animals)
   gathered about us.
By the power of your love,
   enable him or her (them) to live according to
   your plan.
May we always praise you for all your beauty in creation.
Blessed are you, Lord our God, in all your creatures.
Amen.

For One or More Sick Creatures

Heavenly Creator,
you made all things for your glory
and made us caretakers of this creature
(these creatures) under our care.
Restore to health and strength this animal
(this pet) that you have entrusted to us.
Keep this animal (this pet)
always under your loving protection.
Blessed are you, Lord God,
And holy is your name for ever and ever. Amen.

For an Animal That Has Died or Is About to Die

Loving God,

our beloved pet and companion, (name),

    is on its final journey.

We will miss (name) dearly

    because of the joy and affection

    (name) has given to us.

Bless (name) and give him/her peace.

May your care for (name) never die.

We thank you for the gift

    that (name) has been to us.

Give us hope that in your great kindness

    you may restore (name) in your heavenly kingdom

    according to your wisdom, which goes

    beyond our human understanding. Amen.

1
And It Was Very Good

In the earliest verses of Genesis, darkness covered everything until God created light to separate the darkness from the light. "And God saw that the light was good."

Soon we read that God separated the earth from the seas. "And God saw that it was good." Then God added vegetation, plants, trees, and fruit. "And God saw that it was good." On the fourth day, God put two great lights in the sky: the greater light to rule the day and the lesser light to rule the night, thus separating light from darkness. "And God saw that it was good." These two great lights, which St. Francis would call "Brother Sun" and "Sister Moon," have contributed enormously to the well-being and enjoyment of God's creatures.

On the fifth day, God created sea monsters and birds of all kinds. "And God saw that it was good." On the sixth day, God made land creatures of every kind: "cattle and creeping things and wild animals of the earth of every kind. And God saw that it was good." Also on the sixth day, God made human beings, saying, "Let us make humankind in our image, according to our likeness; and let them have dominion over the fish of the sea, and over the birds of the air, and over the cattle, and over all the wild animals of the earth."

Finally, in Genesis 1:31, "God saw everything that he had made, and indeed, it was very good." This "very good" label, which God places upon both human and nonhuman creatures, seems to be an argument for God's desire to have *both* classes of creatures share in the original Garden of Paradise, where peace and harmony reigned between God and human beings, upon creature and creature. Certainly, God is not going to create—and then ignore—what he perceives as "very good" creatures!

God does *everything* out of love, and this includes the creation of our world. God's words to the people of Israel in Jeremiah 31:3 also come to mind: "I have loved you with an everlasting love." The Psalms, too, remind us that God's "steadfast love endures forever." In Psalm 136 alone, the refrain "his steadfast love endures forever" is repeated twenty-five times.

Our God is a God of overflowing love, goodness, and beauty who is ready to give over everything to those he loves. This goodness is reflected in the whole family of creation. When God says of any creature, whether human or nonhuman, that it is "good" or "very good," it is not simply a matter of moral goodness. The creature also has an inherent goodness and beauty—a beauty that reflects God, who is Beauty itself. Surely the Creator would not suddenly stop loving and caring for the creatures he had put into existence with so much care.

2
The Happiness Principle

In the original picture we have of the Garden of Eden before the fall, Adam and Eve and all the creatures are living together happily in peace and harmony in the presence of a loving God—a wonderful and insightful glimpse of the paradise that is to come.

It makes sense to me that the same loving Creator who arranged for these animals and other nonhuman creatures to enjoy happiness in the original Garden would not want to exclude them from the *final* paradise. If they were happy and enjoying God's presence, according to their abilities, in that first Garden, God would want them to be happy and enjoy the same in the restored garden.

Father Don Miller, a Franciscan colleague of mine, recently told me a sad story from his childhood. Don's dog Boots, a young German Shepherd, was tragically killed by a car he had been chasing.

"I was devastated," recalls Don, who was nine years old at the time. "On the verge of tears, I asked my parents: 'Is Boots in heaven and will I see him there some day?'

"This little episode happened in Peoria, Illinois, and my parents took me downtown to Sacred Heart Church to talk with Father Baldwin Schulte, the Franciscan pastor there. I asked Fr. Baldwin whether I would see Boots in heaven. He thought for a moment, and then he turned to me and said: 'Yes, you will see your dog in heaven—if that is what it takes to make you happy.'"

Don reflects, "Now as I look back as an adult, I believe Fr. Baldwin's answer was very wise. Instead of giving me a lot of theology, he basically said that in heaven God will see to it that all who live there are supremely happy. It was a very sound and sensitive answer for me at that time. Once we pass on to the next life and see God face to face, as the glorious source of all that exists, those kinds of questions may not seem so important."

Just as the original Creation was very good with animals as a part of it, so too, it seems, our future lives will be very good and will include animals. No one should presume to tell you or me that we will never again see our pets that died many years ago.

I recall learning in my theology classes that in God there is no past, present, or future. There is only an "eternal now." Who can say, therefore, that the God who created all things does not hold in memory all the creatures God has ever made? They were created as good, all of creation was very good together, and there's no reason why that should change in the eternal future.

The creation story in Genesis says nothing about the future, only about those initial moments when all things were made. But we wonder what will happen in the afterlife—in the new heaven and the new earth that is to come? This is a big-time mystery. There are many things about our future paradise that surpass human understanding. We simply do not know what awaits us in heaven. As St. Paul tells the Corinthians, "We teach what scripture calls: *the things that no eye has seen and no ear has heard, things beyond the mind of man, all that God has prepared for those who love him*" (1 Cor. 2:9 JB).

The Garden of Eden is not only a story of the way the world was created; it is also a metaphor for the final paradise that our loving Creator envisioned before time began.

3
Blessing the Animals

When I try to visualize the final paradise in which animals and humans live together in peace and harmony, I often think of animal blessings that I have taken part in. This is particularly true on the Feast Day of St. Francis, when churches all over the world hold "Blessing of the Animals" services, in which creatures are invited into the sanctuary and offered special blessings as members of God's family. An ideal alternative setting for such a ceremony is a park or a church courtyard with lots of trees and flowers in it and perhaps a fountain or a pool of water.

Ironically, when people bring their pets from different parts of town, there can be disharmony and trouble. Dogs start barking at cats and people struggle to keep animals from fighting, growling, and hissing. But often in my experience, once the blessings begin, a spirit of harmony and peace prevails among pets and people.

Many Christians believe that nonhuman creatures do not have a place in heaven. The reasoning seems to go like this: life with God after death is only possible for human beings who have received the gift of new life with God through baptism. Only humans have intelligence and free will and thus have the capacity to enjoy fullness of life in heaven. Similarly, animals and other nonhuman creatures do not have human souls and are thus excluded from heaven, according to this mindset.

My comment is this: when we consider the story of Adam and Eve before their disobedience, and we look at the animals, the birds, the fish, the trees and plants in the Garden of Eden, they all seem to be in harmonious and happy relationship with God and with Adam and Eve.

True, the nonhuman creatures do not have human souls, but they obviously have some kind of principle of life in order to do the things they do. An animal that shows affection and loyalty, for example, surely has some kind of "soul" or inner light that allows it to enjoy life and give great joy to its caretakers. A bird that sings a beautiful melody contributes to the world of art and, by reflecting the beauty of its Maker, gives us a bit of heaven in the process. There are a lot of things we just don't know about life with God, and one of these things is how nonhumans participate in that life.

One thing we *do* know from the Genesis stories is that animals, plants, and other creatures found happiness in the first Paradise. Why then would God—or anyone else—want to exclude them from the paradise that is yet to come? Just as we find clues in the book of Genesis that God wants animals and other nonhuman creatures to share such joys, so we will also, in the chapters ahead, find clues in other books of Scripture, and elsewhere, that reveal this same desire on the part of God.

For more than thirty-six years, I have worked as a writer and editor for *St. Anthony Messenger*, a national Catholic magazine published by the Franciscan friars of Cincinnati. In our July 2003 issue, we printed an article that I wrote entitled "Will I See My Little Doggy in Heaven?" The article generated a lively reaction from our readers, and we received a larger than usual number of letters, suggesting that the topic of animals in heaven is a live one. I am happy to share with you a letter published two months later in our September issue of that year:

Dear editors:

I am still jumping up and down over the article about animals in heaven. All observations made by Father Jack are sound references to the fact that God loves all creation and will include all in our heavenly home.

For the past several years, I have organized a "Blessing of the Animals." In 1972, I had written to Mother Teresa [of Calcutta] to ask for a letter of support. She sent one, over her own signature, and I quote: "[Animals] too are created by the same hand of God which created us. As we humans are gifted with intelligence, which the animals lack, it is our duty to protect them and to promote their well-being. We also owe it to them as they serve us with such docility and loyalty."

I think Mother Teresa says all there is to say about the sacredness of the animal kingdom.

From Marlene,
Louisville, KY

4
Noah, the Ark, and the Dove

The story of Noah and the ark is simple—it couldn't be more familiar, could it? Most of us knew it as very young children. But our understanding grows, just as our bodies do.

The ark is a wonderful symbol of God's desire to save the whole family of creation. This story makes it apparent that God's plan is not to save humankind apart from other creatures. We are all in the same boat! As St. Paul writes to the Romans (8:22 NAB), "All creation is groaning" for its liberation.

Because of the widespread wickedness at that time, God tells Noah that he is going to destroy everything living on the earth as well as the earth itself. God instructs Noah to build a huge ark with a roof, three decks, a door on the side, and many other specifications.

I am amazed at God's care and solicitude for *all* the creatures in the ark, and this applies to the animals also. God shows his love and care in bringing aboard the ark "every kind" of creature (wanting no species to go extinct) and that they should be "male and female" alike (insuring the continuation and propagation of each of these species). God doesn't want Noah to pack them in the back of a big truck and rush them off to some safe place. No, God wants Noah to be more caring about the details, as well as about all these brother and sister creatures.

"Then the Lord said to Noah, 'Go into the ark, you and all your household, for I have seen that you alone are righteous before me in this generation'" (Gen. 7:1). When we stop to see what's happening, we find that God's care focuses not only upon the human family but also upon the whole family of creation. The animals and other creatures are now part of Noah's "household" and in his care, just as they had been under God's loving care from the beginning. To imitate the broad solicitude of our Creator, a good human leader must care not only for other human beings, but also for the earth and for the wider family of creation.

As children who have heard the story well know, it rained for forty days and forty nights. We also recall that after the rain stopped, Noah opened the window of the ark and sent out a dove to see if the waters had subsided, but since the dove had no place to land, it returned to the ark. Noah waited seven days, and sent the dove out again. This time the dove came back in the evening with an olive leaf. This assured Noah that the waters were subsiding. After waiting another seven days, he sent out the dove, and this time the dove did not return, indicating that the flood was over. Noah and his wife and their three sons and their wives—and all the animals—had survived. All were safe.

But take a closer look at that dove. The episode of Noah and the dove is a little story within the bigger story, and reinforces the idea that God's plan is not to save the humans apart from the other creatures. Humans and other creatures are actually meant to help one another reach our common salvation. What might it mean, if we came to understand humans and animals as helping each other on the way to union with God?

5
Animals and God's Will

We can find many other instances in the Bible (and in our own lives) in which God's creatures collaborate with us in our journey toward salvation and in carrying out God's designs. Consider, for example, the donkey in the Gospels that carried Christ during his triumphal entry into Jerusalem (see Lk. 19:29–38).

Or think of an occasion in your own life—when you see a beautiful flower on a spring day, for example, and it lifts your heart to praise your Creator.

Or consider how often in the book of Psalms the psalmist, upon seeing the sun and moon and shining stars and other beautiful creatures, is inspired to invite these creatures to join the human family in singing God's praises, drawing us all closer to our Creator and our God-given destiny (see Ps. 148).

But let's get back to the bigger story of Noah. That story is not yet finished, even though the flood has gone away. After the waters subsided and dried up, Noah's household, along with all the other creatures, left the ark.

Then Noah built an altar to the Lord, and took of every clean animal and of every clean bird, and offered burnt offerings on the altar. And when the Lord smelled the pleasing odor, the Lord said in his heart, "I will never again curse the ground because

of humankind . . . nor will I ever again destroy every
living creature as I have done." (Gen. 8:20–21)

At this point, "God blessed Noah and his sons, and said
to them, 'Be fruitful and multiply, and fill the earth'" (Gen.
9:1). Interestingly, this is exactly what God told the first
man and woman immediately after God created them "in his
image" in Genesis 1. Apparently, God is telling Noah and his
sons (and their wives, obviously) that this is a "new creation"
and a "second chance."

This time God backs up his pledge, to never again
destroy human beings and other living creatures, with a
solemn covenant. Note that the covenant is made not only
with Noah and his descendants but also *with the other living
creatures*, the animals and birds that had been on the ark. This
suggests that those other creatures communicate with God,
in their own ways, in ways that may be similar and equivalent
to our own communications.

In God's own words, "I establish my covenant with you,
that never again shall all flesh be cut off by the waters of a

flood, and never again shall there be a flood to destroy the earth" (Gen. 9:11). As if to show how serious this pledge is, God introduces a dramatic sign—the rainbow. "God said, 'This is the sign of the covenant that I make between me and you and every living creature that is with you, for all future generations: I have set my bow in the clouds, and it shall be a sign between me and the earth'" (Gen. 9:12–13).

Thus in the story of Noah and the ark, there is no way to mistake that God's plan is to save the human family along with the rest of creation. And God backs this plan up with a covenant—which specifically includes "every living creature." God punctuates this pledge with the rainbow, a sign of hope, arching across the whole family of creation.

6
Jonah and the Whale

Do you remember the story? There is a furious storm at sea. The sailors throw Jonah into the raging water when they discover that Jonah caused the storm. The seas calm. There is a lesson to be "taken away" from the story into our lives.

Jonah had tried to run far away from the task God had asked of him: to preach to the city of Nineveh, the capital city of the Assyrians. The Assyrians were the longtime enemies of the Israelites. It is no surprise then that the Israelites, Jonah among them, felt very little love for the Ninevites. Jonah was not at all pleased that God's saving love included the likes of them. (You may find it interesting to know that the ruins of ancient Nineveh can still be seen today across the Tigris River opposite Mosul in northern Iraq.)

God arranged for a big fish to swallow Jonah. He was in the belly of the fish "three days and three nights." He pleaded for the Lord to deliver him. He offered thanks and pledged obedience to the Lord, saying, "'What I have vowed I will pay. Deliverance belongs to the Lord!' Then the Lord spoke to the fish, and it spewed Jonah out upon the dry land" (2:9–10).

The story of Jonah is a parable of God's all-embracing love. It is amazing to realize that once again *even the animals are included in God's saving plan.* When Jonah proclaimed to the people of Nineveh, "Forty days more and Nineveh will be overthrown," the people and the king of Nineveh were very responsive. "[The king] rose from his throne, removed his robe, covered himself with sackcloth [rough clothing], and sat in ashes" (3:6). Then the king made a decree: "No human being or animal, no herd or flock, shall taste anything. They shall not feed, nor shall they drink water. Human beings and animals shall be covered in sackcloth, and they shall cry mightily to God. All shall turn from their evil ways and from the violence that is in their hands" (3:7–8).

When God saw that the people *and* the animals turned from their evil ways, God changed his mind about the calamity that was to befall the city and withheld all punishment. Jonah became very angry because God's mercy and forgiveness extended beyond the chosen people and included their enemies, the people of Nineveh. Jonah confessed that it was precisely the idea of God's merciful and inclusive love that drove him to flee from God's request that he preach to the people of Nineveh in the first place. Now, no doubt, it made Jonah angrier to know that God wanted to save *even the animals*.

Jonah then went outside the city and made a hut for himself. He sat there waiting to see what would happen to the city. God, meanwhile, provided a bush for Jonah to help shade his head. For this Jonah was grateful. But the next day God had a worm attack the bush, causing it to wither. When the sun rose and beat down on Jonah's head, Jonah asked that he might die, saying, "It is better for me to die than to live" (4:8).

God asked Jonah whether it is right for him "to be angry about the bush." Jonah replied, "Yes, angry enough to die" (4:9). To this the Lord replied,

> You are concerned about the bush, for which you did not labor and which you did not grow; it came into being in a night and perished in a night. And should I not be concerned about Nineveh, that great city, in which there are more than a hundred and twenty thousand persons who do not know their right hand from their left, and also many animals?" (4:10–11).

This intriguing question ends the story: God's point seems to be that, if Jonah can throw a big snit about a little bush for which Jonah did not even lift his little finger, why should not the loving Creator of the universe be concerned about the great city of Nineveh and all the human beings and animals that live there?

Just as in the story of Noah and the ark, when a dove was used by Noah to assist in God's plan to save the whole family of creation, so now in this amazing, inspired story of Jonah, we see a big fish taking a similar role. The fish plays a key function in helping the reluctant Jonah carry out God's plan to save Nineveh. Again, this is an example of a creature helping us on our way to salvation. We are a part of the Creation, not *apart from* it.

God uses a bush and a worm to lead the narrow-minded Jonah to a better understanding of the inclusive nature of God's saving love. Human beings and other creatures are meant to help each other in our common journey toward our future life with God.

Animals can teach us a lot about rising above our narrow-mindedness and intolerance. We see dogs, cats, and other pets showing great affection to their owners, whether these owners be rich or poor, black or white, beautiful or disfigured, healthy or sick. I have a clear memory of a volunteer coming regularly to a nursing home a few years ago with a young Collie to visit my mother and other residents of that home. That dog certainly gave great comfort to my mom, who was coping with cancer at the time. The dog, with the full approval of the volunteer, had no qualms whatsoever about lying alongside my ninety-four-year-old mother as she lay propped up in bed. She was so happy to pet and enjoy this wonderful creature on her final journey toward life with God.

We have much to learn about God's inclusive love, and about *our* role in collaborating respectfully with other creatures as we go on our way to fulfill our Creator's holy designs.

7
Creatures Praise Our Creator

In the book of Psalms we find prayers in which human beings invite other creatures to praise God along with them. The clear impression in these prayers is that the nonhuman creatures are meant to participate in our prayerful journey into the presence of God. These are often inclusive prayers addressed to a wide range of God's creation: sun and moon, trees, animals, birds, sea monsters, as well as to a variety of people.

Psalm 148 is a dramatic example of this. In the New American Bible (1986 edition), this psalm bears the awesome title: "Hymn of All Creation to the Almighty Creator." I invite you to read—or better, to pray—this hymn, which includes a broad spectrum of God's creatures:

PSALM 148

Hymn of All Creation to the Almighty Creator

I. Praise the LORD from the heavens;
praise him in the heights.
Praise him, all you angels;
praise him, all you his host.
Praise him, sun and moon;
praise him, all you shining stars.
Praise him, you highest heavens,
and you waters above the heavens.

Let them praise the name of the LORD,

for he commanded and they were created;

He established them forever and ever;

he gave them a duty which shall not pass away.

II. Praise the LORD from the earth,

you sea monsters and all depths;

Fire and hail, snow and mist,

storm winds that fulfill his word;

You mountains and all you hills,

you fruit trees and all you cedars;

You wild beasts and all tame animals,

you creeping things and you winged foul.

III. Let the kings of the earth and all peoples,

the princes and all the judges of the earth,

Young men too, and maidens,

old men and boys,

Praise the name of the LORD,

for his name alone is exalted;

His majesty is above earth and heaven,

and he has lifted up the horn of his people.
Be this his praise from all his faithful ones,
from the children of Israel, the people close to him.
Alleluia. (NAB 1986)

In the first two stanzas, nonhuman creatures in heaven, sea, and earth are praising God. And in the final stanza, those praising God are all human beings. The picture we have is of the combined family of creation joined in praising God together. Doesn't that seem to be the way that God wills it? God is not seeking praise solely from the *human* part of the family, but from the *whole* family of creation.

Just as in the story of the ark and the great flood, in which Noah and his family along with the larger family of nonhuman creatures are saved together, so it is in the case of this hymn. All creatures are praising God together. *We are all in the same boat*, once again, seeking a share in God's mercy and love, and someday, final happiness in the restored garden.

8
The Song of St. Francis

The broad strokes of his life are familiar to most. St. Francis was born in 1182 in the Umbrian town of Assisi. The son of a prosperous cloth merchant, Francis was a carefree and generous youth.

His companions dubbed him the "King of Revels." He loved the good life and partying with his friends. All the while, however, he dreamed of becoming a knight and achieving glory on the battlefield. The opportunity soon arrived and Francis rode off as a knight of Assisi to fight against the neighboring town of Perugia.

Assisi, however, was roundly defeated in its very first skirmish, and Francis was captured and became a prisoner of war. It was a bitter blow for this idealistic young man of twenty-one. Francis spent a year in prison and returned home to Assisi a broken man.

Yet a plan seemed to be unfolding. While praying alone one day before a crucifix in the abandoned chapel of San Damiano located down the hill from Assisi, Francis heard these words coming from the cross: "Francis, repair my house, which is falling into ruin." The saint realized only later that it was a larger house, the Christian Church itself, that Christ was calling him to rebuild.

Another dramatic sign of Francis's new direction came through his meeting with a leper on the road. Francis was inspired to dismount his horse and warmly embrace and kiss the leper. Later Francis confessed in his *Testament* that "[w]hat had seemed bitter to me [an encounter with leprosy] was turned into sweetness of soul and body." Francis realized that he had actually embraced his Lord, Jesus Christ.

Soon Francis found himself living among lepers and humbly caring for them. Others, seeing Francis joyfully ministering to the lepers and to other outcasts, asked to join Francis in his ministry to the poor. These followers would soon grow into a brotherhood, and in 1209, Pope Innocent III approved the Franciscan way of life.

But this early information about the life of St. Francis does not tell us about another very important aspect of Francis's life, namely his great admiration for the wonders of nature and the marvelous creatures God placed on earth to accompany us on our journey to God. This brings us to St. Francis's great *Canticle of the Creatures*. This hymn, or song of praise to our Creator, was composed very much in the spirit of Psalm 148 discussed in the previous chapter.

This song is also known as *The Canticle of Brother Sun.* In it Francis gives the title of "Brother" and "Sister" to the various creatures, emphasizing as best he could that we all form *one family of creation* under one loving "Father." "Sister" and "Brother," of course, are familial terms that people formerly only used for fellow humans.

Francis had a strong sense, which he probably learned from the Old Testament psalms and hymns, that we are not meant to journey to God alone, in proud isolation from our brother and sister creatures. Indeed, Francis would have regularly encountered these psalms and hymns in his liturgical prayers. For example, he would have certainly recited with frequency the following verses from the book of Daniel:

Sun and moon, bless the Lord;
    praise and exalt him above all forever.
Stars of heaven, bless the Lord;
    praise and exalt him above all forever.
Every shower and dew, bless the Lord;
    praise and exalt him above all forever.

All you winds, bless the Lord;

    praise and exalt him above all forever.

Fire and heat, bless the Lord;

    praise and exalt him above all forever. (3:62–66 NAB)

One can easily imagine Francis borrowing these words and phrases and using them in his *Canticle of the Creatures*. Just as in the case of the psalms and hymns of the Hebrew Scriptures, Francis invites us in his exuberant *Canticle* to form one family with these creatures and to sing out in one symphony of praise to our common Creator.

Here is a slightly condensed version of St. Francis's famous song:

The Canticle of the Creatures

Most high, all-powerful, all-good Lord!

    All praise is yours, all glory, all honor,

    and all blessing.

To you alone, Most High, do they belong.

    No mortal lips are worthy

    to pronounce your name.

All praise be yours, my Lord,
  through all that you have made,
And first my lord Brother Sun,
    who brings the day;
    and light you give to us through him.
    How beautiful is he,
    how radiant in all his splendor!
    Of you, Most High, he bears the likeness.
All praise be yours, my Lord,
  through Sister Moon and Stars,
    in the heavens you have made them, bright
    and precious and fair.
All praise be yours, my Lord,
  through Brothers Wind and Air,
    and fair and stormy, all the weather's moods,
    by which you cherish all that you have made.
All praise be yours, my Lord, through Sister Water,
  so useful, lowly, precious, and pure.

All praise be yours, my Lord, through Brother Fire,

    through whom you brighten up the night.

    How beautiful is he, how merry!

    Full of power and strength.

All praise be yours, my Lord,

   through Sister Earth, our mother,

    who feeds us in her sovereignty and produces

    various fruits and colored flowers and herbs. . . .

Praise and bless my Lord, and give him thanks,

    And serve him with great humility.

9
St. Francis and the Creatures

Just as we find a spirit of great care and reverence for the creatures in St. Francis's *Canticle*, so we find in Francis's daily life the same spirit of reverence for every creature he encountered along his way.

Francis's care for creation even extended to earthworms he saw on the roadway. He would carefully pick them up and place them on the side of the road where they would be out of harm's way. Francis saw the goodness and beauty of God in the sunset or in a gurgling stream. He was in awe of the butterfly as well as the cricket.

"Where the modern cynic sees something 'bug-like' in everything that exists," observed the German writer-philosopher Max Scheler, "St. Francis saw even in a bug the sacredness of life."

There are many other popular stories about St. Francis and other creatures.

One day a rabbit was brought to him by a brother who had found it caught in a trap. Francis admonished the rabbit to be more careful in the future. Releasing the rabbit from the trap, Francis sat it on the ground and told it to go its way. But the rabbit just hopped back to Francis and sat on his lap, desiring to stay close to him. Francis carried the rabbit into the woods and set it free. The rabbit simply followed Francis back to where he was seated and jumped onto his lap again.

Finally Francis asked one of his brothers to take the rabbit deep into the forest and let it go. This time it worked; the rabbit remained content there. Such episodes were always happening to Francis, who saw this as an opportunity to give praise to God.

Francis also made friends with fish. Once, he was crossing a lake with a fisherman, who caught a nice-sized fish and gave it to Francis as a gift. Francis, however, simply warned the fish not to get caught again and placed it back in the water.

This brings us to the well-known legend of Francis and a fierce wolf that had been terrorizing the village of Gubbio. The wolf had attacked and even killed some of the townspeople. Through the intervention of Francis, the townspeople promised to feed the wolf, if the wolf stopped its violent attacks. Francis brought the conflict to a peaceful solution. He was the sort of person—extraordinarily rare but possible—who could communicate with creatures, because he was sensitive to them and to their needs.

Finally we have the famous story of Francis's preaching to the birds. Sometimes people hear this story out of its proper context. This episode was not a fanciful event. We shouldn't make it into something magical, unrelated to real life.

In reading the story again recently, I was puzzled by the way that Francis's biographer St. Bonaventure positioned this famous story in his *Life of St. Francis*. He placed the story right at the point in Francis's life where he is struggling with a deep personal dilemma: should he retire from the world and devote himself entirely to prayer, or should he continue traveling about as a preacher of the gospel? To answer this question, Francis sent brothers to seek the advice of two trusted colleagues: Brother Sylvester and St. Clare. Word came back quickly from both Sylvester and Clare that it was their clear judgment that God wanted Francis to keep proclaiming the Good News of God's saving love. No sooner did Francis hear their response than he immediately stood up, and in the words of Bonaventure, "without the slightest delay he took to the roads to carry out the divine command" with great fervor.

We might expect Francis to go running off to the nearest village to begin preaching the gospel to the people gathered there. But where does Francis actually go? His very next stop, according to Bonaventure, is this: "He came to a spot where a large flock of birds of various kinds had come together. When God's saint saw them, he quickly ran to the spot and greeted them as if they were endowed with reason. . . ."

He went right up to them and solicitously urged them to listen to the word of God, saying, "Oh birds, my brothers [and sisters], you have a great obligation to praise your Creator, who clothed you in feathers and gave you wings to fly with, provided you with pure air and cares for you without any worry on your part. . . ." The birds showed their joy in a remarkable fashion: They began to stretch their necks, extend their wings, open their beaks, and gaze at him attentively.

He went through their midst with amazing fervor of spirit, brushing against them with his tunic. Yet none of them moved from the spot until the man of God made the sign of the cross and gave them permission to leave; then they all flew away together. His companions waiting on the road saw all these things. When he returned to them, that pure and simple man began to accuse himself of negligence because he had not preached to the birds before.

During his life, St. Francis had more than one mystical experience in which Jesus revealed himself as a God of overflowing goodness and love who would lay down his own life for Francis. The same incredible goodness that Francis saw in God he saw also in creatures. That is why he could compose a *Canticle of the Creatures* that not only praises the Creator as good in its opening line ("Most high, all-powerful, all-good Lord!") but also describes the creatures with similar words: "beautiful," "radiant," "bright," "precious and fair"— words shining with the glory and goodness of God.

Francis's amazement at God's goodness is reflected time and again in his style of prayer. In a prayer from his *Praises before the Office,* Francis suddenly begins repeating, if not babbling, the word *good,* as if intoxicated by it. He prays:

All powerful, all holy, most high and supreme God,

sovereign good, all good,

every good, you who alone

are good, it is to you we must give all praise,

all glory, all thanks, all honor, all blessing;

to you we must refer

all good always. Amen.

Artists, too, have often expressed this kind of goodness and reverence in their artistic representations of St. Francis and his fellow creatures. I think of the great painter Giotto and his famous thirteenth-century fresco of *St. Francis Preaching to the Birds* that is located in the Upper Basilica of St. Francis in Assisi. In this painting, Francis and another friar companion are standing in front of a tree and a large group of birds are scattered on the ground before Francis and looking intently toward him. Francis's right hand is raised in blessing as he bends slightly before them in a posture of gentle reverence and wonder before the mystery of God's creation. The whole scene exudes a sense of the goodness of God.

I think also of present-day artists who have sculpted popular statues of St. Francis that stand in our flower gardens or on our birdbaths. I think of greeting cards and T-shirts showing images of Francis with birds flying around his head or with a rabbit in his arms. Such images inspire us to love and respect all creatures.

St. Francis addressed creatures as "sisters" and "brothers," that is, as equals, not as subjects to be dominated. That is why the humble figure of St. Francis standing on the birdbath or among the shrubs is so right for our day. He truly saw himself as a simple servant and a caretaker of creation—little brother to the birds and the fish and the lowly ivy.

For these reasons and more, Pope John Paul II proclaimed St. Francis of Assisi the patron of ecology in 1979. The pope cited him for being "an example of genuine and deep respect for the integrity of creation." "St. Francis," he added, "invited all creation—animals, plants, natural forces, even Brother Sun and Sister Moon—to give honor and praise to the Lord."

10
Jesus and the World of Creation

Jesus of Nazareth lived his earthly life twelve centuries before St. Francis of Assisi. Long before Francis understood a sense of brotherhood with the rest of creation, Jesus had plunged in and immersed himself in the created world,

becoming a *brother to every creature.* This he did through the
Incarnation—a breathtaking event that sent rumblings of
new life and hope through the entire network of creation.

The Incarnation is the central mystery of Christianity.
One thing is very clear: Jesus, as the Divine Word, did not
hold himself aloof from the world he had come to save, but
literally and wholeheartedly *entered* the family of creation. He
did this through his incarnation, his taking human form, his
birth at Bethlehem. It's an amazing mystery, because when
the Word became flesh in Christ and made his home among
us, not only were human beings raised to a new and glorious
dignity but all other creatures were as well.

When Jesus walked this earth, he must have perceived
that the whole world had been ennobled by his entering into
it. Jesus felt at home on this earth, whether on the lakeshore
or in the desert, whether walking down a mountainside or
crossing a wheat field or sailing across the Sea of Galilee.

In his preaching of the Good News, Jesus delighted in
using images from nature, such as the birds of the air and
the lilies of the field. He populated his sermons with stories

of foxes, pearls, salt, yeast, fig trees, mustard seed, weeds and wheat, moths, and lost sheep. He understood from his profound knowledge of Scripture that all these creatures were blessed and pronounced *good* by the Creator in the beginning.

Jesus used many created things in his saving work, such as wet clay to heal the eyes of a blind man. He used bread and wine, the product of wheat and grapes, to represent his very presence in the Eucharist. We see from examples like this how Jesus incorporated other creatures into his mission of carrying out God's saving plan for the world.

Finally, near the end of Mark's Gospel, in his farewell message to his disciples, Jesus left a strong hint that the whole family of creation was to be included in God's saving work. After his death and resurrection, Jesus tells his disciples: "Go into the whole world and proclaim the gospel to every creature" (Mk. 16:15). Mark does not use the words "to every human being," but "to every creature." Jesus' choice of words suggests that the gospel message will have a saving impact upon the *whole* family of creation, and not simply on the human family.

11
Praying with Creatures

Coming as I do from the Roman Catholic tradition, my fellow worshipers and I are used to liturgies of prayer that rely heavily on a wide and rich spectrum of creatures. On our most solemn feasts, for example, we use fire, clouds of incense, blazing candles, and multicolored flowers.

In our sacramental celebrations, we use bread, wine, water, oil, ashes, and palm branches. We decorate our prayer spaces with stained glass windows, images of lambs, doves, lions, eagles, oxen, and asses. We pray in the company of these creatures day after day in our public worship.

As a Catholic I find it normal to incorporate these brother and sister creatures into my worship. Sacramentality is very much the air we breathe, whether it is a matter of celebrating the Eucharist or public prayers that mention our fellow creatures. Christians of all backgrounds can believe in the inherent sanctity of all these creatures, accepting them as outward signs and "sacraments" of God's presence, goodness, and grace.

One of the prayers we frequently hear the priest say at Mass is:

Father, you are holy indeed and all
creation rightly gives you praise.

I love this prayer. The words express our way of including the whole family of creation in prayer. We can surely find new ways to apply these words to the creatures we invite to accompany us in praising God.

There is a principle in Catholic theology that goes like this in Latin: *lex orandi, lex credendi.* Translated literally, it means, "The law of prayer is the law of belief." An easier-to-understand translation would be:

The way we pray indicates
the way we believe.

May we find more and creative words to express what we believe about this world, and the one to come.

12
The Soul of a Dog

The question—"Will I see my dog (my cat, my rabbit, my gerbil, my parrot, my turtle) in heaven?"—is one that is very close to our hearts. It is important. The question of the future of our beloved pets holds deep emotional importance for us—and it should.

Although I do not have a dog or a pet at this point in my life, I have some experience of caring for animals and feeling emotional ties to them. Let me tell you a story that takes me back many years.

Around 1943, when I was about eight years old, our family had a dog named Toppy, and my older brother, Paul, and I had the responsibility of taking care of him. Toppy was part Beagle and was under our care only for a year or two, because it wasn't long before the poor creature got hit and killed by a car. My brother witnessed the tragic event and ran into our house, crying inconsolably, telling the rest of us the terrible news. I keenly felt that loss.

For weeks and maybe months after his death, I kept expecting to see Toppy come bounding into our backyard where his doghouse had stood—but Toppy never showed up. Obviously, that strong memory, still vividly with me so many years later, is a clear indication of my own grief. So I understand how difficult it is to lose such a loved one.

Let me tell you a more recent story, as well. Magic is a different dog and a different story altogether. Magic came into my life more recently. Her home is in Seattle, Washington, with my sister and brother-in-law, Tese and Bill Neighbor, and their two teenage boys, Josh and Noah. Magic is a Golden Retriever. I knew Magic as a pup, and my fondness for her is renewed often, thanks to visits with the family in Seattle at Christmastime, and sometimes in the summer as well.

About eight years ago the Neighbors invited me to use their cabin while I was working on a writing project. Their cabin is located on the Olympic Peninsula, two or three hours west of Seattle. Tese persuaded me that during my two- or three-week stay at the cabin I might want to babysit for Magic, who was just a pup at the time. Her request had its perks. The cabin with its ample deck sits on a wooded hillside and has a panoramic view of the Hood Canal, part of the intercoastal water system that spreads out from Seattle. The area is rich in natural beauty and wildlife. Two bald eagles often perch atop a tall pine tree that towers over the cabin. Those awesome birds seem to have almost come with the property.

To breathe in all this beauty and bond with this affectionate pup were great blessings for me. Besides feeding and watching over Magic, I took breaks from my writing project and went on happy walks with her on scenic forest paths along the canal.

As time went on, Magic began living up to her name as a *retriever*. She displayed incredible retrieving skills at the cabin. Somehow Magic learned to retrieve bright green tennis balls thrown off the cabin deck toward the canal that spreads out like a huge lake down below. The cabin's deck must be sixty feet above the surface of the water. To get to the water, Magic had to race down fifteen or so wooden steps connecting the deck to the ground below, then charge some twenty yards down the steep hillside through the shrubs and undergrowth, down twenty more wooden steps to the level of the canal—and finally dash another few yards to reach the water. During one of my summer visits about a decade ago, Magic came to me with a tennis ball clenched in her teeth and dropped it at my feet on the deck, then looked up at me with her bright eyes, as if to say, "Try me out!"

Having played baseball as a teenager, I still have a fairly good arm. After warming up a bit, I threw the ball over the top branches of a row of tall evergreens that partially blocked the view of the canal from spectators on the deck, including

Magic. Magic watched my wind-up and throw quite carefully. Then, after catching only a split-second glimpse of the ball's trajectory, she charged down the steps and hillside and soon plunged into the water below. Amazingly, within two or three minutes she came rushing back onto the deck and dropped the ball at my feet. She looked up at me again with her bright eyes and playful grin. This girl really loves being a retriever, I thought with amazement. And as I soon found out, Magic could keep playing this game for hours.

Happily, another very appealing dog has come into my life within the last year or so—a little white Shih Tzu named Tita. She's as cute as a button and is often a guest at Pleasant Street Friary in Cincinnati's inner city, where I live with five other Franciscan friars. Tita belongs to a friend of Mark, one of the friars with whom I live, and is with us one or two days a week, or even more when her owner is called out of town. She is a hit with everyone because she brings her own brand of joy and affection into the friary.

Jim, one of the other friars, has taught her a few tricks such as rolling over, extending her paw for a "handshake," and standing on her hind legs to ask for a bit of food. Tita sometimes joins us when our small community of friars gathers for the Eucharist. She is always very quiet and reverent during Mass, and some of us enjoy greeting Tita at the "sign of peace." We are happy to have this wonderful fellow creature "praising God" with us at times in our friary. In her own mysterious and "doggy" way, Tita is a little mirror of the goodness and love of God that we celebrate in the Eucharist.

Then there is one more dog that I feel compelled to tell you about, because he brought great peace to my soul three or four years ago. I was visiting some good friends who introduced me to Pippy, a full-grown, chocolate Labrador Retriever. I was seated when they brought the dog into the room. Rather large, he came up close and sat upright directly in front of me. He just sat there in silence, hardly a foot away from my face, looking into my eyes with an expression of gentle sadness. He did this more than once during my visit.

Quite puzzled by what was going on between Pippy and me, I asked Pippy's owners what they thought was happening. My friends, who knew that my mother had died from cancer two or three weeks earlier, told me that Pippy had probably sensed my emotional pain and felt a sympathetic connection with me. That rang true, because my heart had been deeply wrenched by my mother's death, and I could feel a real flow of compassion coming from Pippy. This is a very comforting memory for me. Pippy just sat there and kept looking at me in silence as if to comfort and to say, "I feel your loss."

I know that some people say animals don't have souls. I have no problem agreeing that they don't have exactly the same kind of souls that humans have. But I have a hard time accepting that an animal like Magic or Tita or Pippy does not have a soul.

All of these dogs that I have known and loved also have great intelligence, and an amazing set of instincts. Nobody can say that they don't have mighty hearts, a wonderful sense of play, and great capacities to give and receive affection.

Even if you have trouble seeing that dogs such as these have souls, I hope that you will at least agree that they have received amazing gifts from our Creator.

13
The
Afterlife

In this book I have set forth reasons why I believe that creatures other than humans will find a place in that "new heaven and new earth" that the Bible talks about.

In the creation accounts of Genesis, we have learned that all creatures are good and reflect the goodness of God. It is easy for me to recognize this same goodness not only in the abstract, but also when I think specifically of Toppy, Magic, Tita, Pippy, and other creatures I've come to know.

I have also discussed how belief in Jesus Christ, who entering our created world through the Incarnation, elevates the dignity not only of humans but also of animals. I find it meaningful to apply this elevated dignity to Magic and Tita and to all of our animal companions. The same is true of the principal of sacramentality—the belief that every created thing can be a sign or "sacrament" of the divine. This can certainly apply to our beloved animal friends.

So, then, what about the resurrection of our bodies and the bodies of our beloved animals? Does it make sense to believe that this will happen? This is part of the Christian's hope for heaven.

I would like to answer this question by sharing with you a quote from St. Paul's letter to the Philippians that very recently caught me by surprise: "Our citizenship is in heaven, and from it we also await a savior, the Lord Jesus Christ. He will change our lowly body to conform with his glorified body by the power that enables him also to bring all things into subjection to himself" (Phil. 3:20–21 NAB).

These words caught me by surprise. Paul is assuring us that our true home ("our citizenship") is in heaven. He assures us that our bodies too are destined to rise again and be transformed like Christ's own body. Paul also tells us that Christ, as the Lord of Creation, is able "to bring all things into subjection to himself." He is saying that our Savior somehow contains "all things" in his risen body. Paul seems to be saying that "all things"—whether human, animal, plant, or mineral—are somehow meant to be saved and summed up in the risen Christ.

If we believe, therefore, in these words of St. Paul and in our wider Judeo-Christian vision, I feel we can make a good case for saying: yes, in some mysterious but real way, our animal, plant, and mineral companions, our "brothers" and "sisters," will be with us in the restored Garden of Eden.

In chapter 5 of the book of Revelation, the inspired writer gives us an intriguing description of a vision he saw when he was a prisoner on the Greek island of Patmos. The vision is reminiscent of Psalm 148, because it gives us a glimpse of all creatures of the universe praising God together.

In his vision, John sees God sitting on a glorious throne in heaven. Standing near the throne is Jesus in the form of a lamb. An immense crowd of angels and human beings are also there before God and the Lamb. Here is John's testimony:

> Then I heard every creature in heaven and on earth and under the earth and in the sea, everything in the universe cry out: "To the one who sits on the throne and to the Lamb be blessing and honor, glory and might, forever and ever." (Rev. 5:13 NAB)

What we see here, in the last book of the Bible, is the whole family of creation praising God and the Lamb. We know that the book of Revelation often communicates its message symbolically rather than literally. Whatever way we look at John's vision, however, he seems to be affirming that all creatures of the universe are in the presence of God, and blessing him with "honor and glory . . . forever and ever."

There are several other places in the book of Revelation where there are hopeful Scripture passages about a future paradise, the state of happiness we commonly call heaven, and they all bring my thoughts back to Pippy, one of the dogs that I have loved so much. Thanks to his compassionate gaze into my eyes, Pippy helped remove some of the pain I was carrying in my heart caused by my mother's death. Pippy connected with me in a profound way that wasn't human, but was creature to creature.

In the new heavens and the new earth, and in the "Peaceable Kingdom" described by the prophet Isaiah, the lion and the lamb and many other creatures live together in happy harmony. One of the themes of this book is that the whole family of creation is meant to walk together in peace and harmony on this earth as we journey to God. I found

Pippy helpful in my own life's journey, in that he made my mother's death easier to bear. Of course, many loving human beings also consoled me in similar ways through their prayers, words, and loving support. Yet, it is consoling to remember that our animal companions are also able to support us in such stressful situations.

There is another image from Revelation that follows immediately after John's vision of "a new heaven and a new earth," and that is the "new Jerusalem."

John writes: "I also saw the holy city, the new Jerusalem, coming down out of heaven from God, prepared as a bride adorned for her husband. I heard a loud voice from the throne saying, 'Behold, God's dwelling is with the human race. He will dwell with them and they will be his people and God himself will always be with them (as their God)'" (Rev. 21:2–3 NAB). This, too, has implications for our hope that we will see our pets in heaven.

The idea expresses an amazingly intense and loving, marriagelike union between God and his people. This intimate union would be a state of happiness not unlike heaven itself. In fact, if we were to die in that kind of union with God, we would indeed be in heaven.

Even now, if we are trying to live our lives out of love for God and according to God's plan, we would be enjoying a heavenlike state, would we not?—or at least a *foretaste* of the heaven still to come?

After announcing, through John, this kind of union between God and the human race, "The one who sat on the throne said, 'Behold, I make all things new'" (Rev. 21:5 NAB). God seems to be going well beyond making all human beings new to say "I make *all things* new." *All things* is the literal translation of the Greek word *panta*. The word is clearly neuter and would refer to all things of creation taken together, including human, animal, plant, and mineral.

The Jerusalem Bible translation is: "Now I am making the whole of creation new." God's saving love includes the whole family of creation, not only the human beings.

14
Conclusion

Jesus once said that we are to have faith like children. Kids can sometimes see and understand those things that we adults, for whatever reasons, no longer seem to see or understand quite as clearly.

Many people whose pets have died have personally told me that they just "know" in their hearts or by some inner intuition that their beloved dog or cat or parrot is in heaven. Children often have a similar instinct or inner sense about their pets and other animals being in heaven.

Jesus once uttered this prayer: "I bless you, Father, Lord of heaven and of earth, for hiding these things from the learned and the clever and revealing them to mere children" (Mt. 11:25 JB). In this spirit, I have something similar to share with you. . . .

Thanks to the kind assistance of a friend, an elementary school teacher in Cincinnati, eight first-grade students offered these brief answers to my question:

"Why should animals go to heaven?"

1. "If they didn't go to heaven, who would take care of them?" (Jackson)

2. "So they can be with their owner who loves them." (Liz)

3. "Because it's the only place for them to go if they are good." (Jakari)

4. "Because they are good." (Nathan)

5. "Because God loves his creations." (Leah)

6. "Because he [God] loves them and wants them to live with him." (Amber)

7. "When it dies, where else would it go?" (Rachel)

8. "If only *people* were in heaven, it would be boring." (Radu)

We may not know exactly how God will bring the whole family of creation some day to heaven. What we do know is this: our faith, supported by Scripture, Christian teaching, and the life and example of St. Francis of Assisi, gives us solid hints and clues that if we live in harmony with God's plans, we will see the "whole of creation" in the world to come.

Does our most holy and good Creator-God need our permission to fill his new heaven and new earth with the whole family of creation? Of course not. Nor did God need our permission to place them in that first primeval Paradise.

This gift of life with God in a new heaven and a new earth comes simply from God's own overflowing love and goodness. What is more, in this restored garden-still-to-come there will be no wall of separation between the holy and the profane, the sacred and the secular. That wall is one that *we* make, and, of course, it does not exist in the eyes of God. In heaven, the holiness of all God's creatures will be apparent. Even though all of us earthly creatures are clearly distinct from God, we will yet, somehow, be one with God and the risen Jesus. "[God] is not far from each one of us," as St. Paul reminded the Athenians. "For 'in him we live and move and have our being'" (Acts 17:27–28).

In the new heaven and new earth God will walk side by side with all of us. "The wolf shall be the guest of the lamb" (Isa. 11:6 NAB), and, hopefully, the fox will live with the rabbit, and we humans will be the happy companions and loving caregivers of our dogs and cats—and all the other creatures.

I have come to believe, "Yes, with heartfelt thanks to God's saving love for the whole family of creation, *I will see my dog in heaven!*"

About Paraclete Press

Who We Are

Paraclete Press is a publisher of books, recordings, and DVDs on Christian spirituality. Our publishing represents a full expression of Christian belief and practice—from Catholic to Evangelical, from Protestant to Orthodox.

We are the publishing arm of the Community of Jesus, an ecumenical monastic community in the Benedictine tradition. As such, we are uniquely positioned in the marketplace without connection to a large corporation and with informal relationships to many branches and denominations of faith.

What We Are Doing

Books | Paraclete publishes books that show the richness and depth of what it means to be Christian. Although Benedictine spirituality is at the heart of all that we do, we publish books that reflect the Christian experience across many cultures, time periods, and houses of worship. We publish books that nourish the vibrant life of the church and its people—books about spiritual practice, formation, history, ideas, and customs.

We have several different series, including the best-selling Paraclete Essentials and Paraclete Giants series of classic texts in contemporary English; Voices from the Monastery—men and women monastics writing about living a spiritual life today; award-winning poetry; best-selling gift books for children on the occasions of baptism and first communion; and the Active Prayer Series that brings creativity and liveliness to any life of prayer.

Recordings | From Gregorian chant to contemporary American choral works, our music recordings celebrate sacred choral music through the centuries. Paraclete distributes the recordings of the internationally acclaimed choir Gloriæ Dei Cantores, praised for their "rapt and fathomless spiritual intensity" by American Record Guide, and the Gloriæ Dei Cantores Schola, which specializes in the study and performance of Gregorian chant. Paraclete is also the exclusive North American distributor of the recordings of the Monastic Choir of St. Peter's Abbey in Solesmes, France, long considered to be a leading authority on Gregorian chant.

Videos | Our videos offer spiritual help, healing, and biblical guidance for life issues: grief and loss, marriage, forgiveness, anger management, facing death, and spiritual formation.

Learn more about us at our website:
www.paracletepress.com,
or call us toll-free at 1-800-451-5006.

SCAN
TO
READ
MORE

You may also be interested in ...

I Will See You in Heaven
CAT LOVER'S EDITION *!*

Friar Jack Wintz

ISBN: 978-1-61261-585-5
$13.99, Trade paper

Yes, you will see your beloved cat again—in heaven! Complete with space for presenting the book to a friend who has lost, or may soon lose, a beloved cat; prayers and blessings for all pets; and plenty of hope and inspiration from Friar Jack.

Will I See My Pet in Heaven?
CHILDREN'S EDITION *!*

Friar Jack Wintz

ISBN: 978-1-61261-098-6
$14.99, Hardcover

This charming book is the children's edition of the Paraclete bestseller, *I Will See You in Heaven* (more than 75,000 copies sold). It comforts and explains to children that God loves and cares for all creatures, including and especially those we are close to. Includes a presentation page for gift-giving.